POPE FRANCIS'
LITTLE BOOK OF
COMPASSION

First published in 2017 by
Hampton Roads Publishing Company, Inc.
Charlottesville, VA 22906
Distributed by Red Wheel/Weiser, LLC
www.redwheelweiser.com

Published by arrangement with HarperCollins*Publishers* Ltd
Copyright © 2017 HarperCollins*Publishers*

Copyright © 2017 by Libreria Editrice Vaticana
Compiled by Andrea Kirk Assaf
Edited by Tony Assaf
Cover design by e-Digital Design
Cover photo credit: Pope Francis addresses the crowd on Easter Sunday, 2013 © Alamy.
Text design by e-Digital Design

ISBN: 978-1-57174-778-5
Library of Congress Cataloging-in-Publication Data available upon request

Printed in China
10 9 8 7 6 5 4 3 2 1

MIX
**Paper from
responsible sources**

FSC
www.fsc.org
FSC™ C007454

FSC™ is a non-profit international organisation established to promote the
responsible management of the world's forests. Products carrying the FSC
label are independently certified to assure consumers that they come from
forests that are managed to meet the social, economic and ecological needs
of present and future generations, and other controlled sources.

Find out more about HarperCollins and the environment at
www.harpercollins.co.uk/green

POPE FRANCIS' LITTLE BOOK OF COMPASSION

The Essential Teachings

Compiled by Andrea Kirk Assaf

HAMPTON ROADS

What does Jesus ask of us? He desires hearts that are truly consecrated, hearts that draw life from His forgiveness in order to pour it out with compassion on our brothers and sisters.

Pope Francis

*C*ontents

A Note from the Editor   11

PART ONE: Compassion through Mercy   23

PART TWO: Compassion through Prayer   73

PART THREE: Compassion through Forgiveness   107

PART FOUR: Compassion through Solidarity   147

PART FIVE: Compassion through Charity and Service   205

PART SIX: Compassion through Hospitality   255

PART SEVEN: Compassion through Jesus   285

PART EIGHT: Pope Francis on Compassion   323

PART NINE: Reader's Journal   337

About the Editors   394

A Note from the Editor

By coincidence, or perhaps Providence, I began to write these words on the Feast of the Transfiguration of Our Lord. The word 'transfiguration' came to my mind as I read and reread the quotes collected in this little book by Pope Francis.

Transfiguration is 'a complete change of form or appearance into a more beautiful or spiritual state.' In Biblical terms, it refers to the transfiguration of Christ before the Apostles Peter, James, and John, as recorded in *Matthew* 17:2, *Mark* 9:2–3, and *Luke* 9:28–36.

In these pages, Pope Francis makes a compelling case for compassionate living as the way in which we become transfigured into true Christians, that is, those who strive to imitate Jesus Christ, the Good Samaritan. It is the standard, Pope Francis says, by which we will ultimately be judged as believers.

Before we can undertake the difficult task of bestowing compassion upon others, however, we must understand the origin of compassion, and know that it has already been bestowed upon us. 'The compassion of God, His suffering with us, gives meaning and worth to our struggles and suffering,' Pope Francis explains. The word 'compassion' derives from two Latin words meaning 'to suffer with.'

Compassion is realized through action, and in this Pope Francis has shown us the way through his tenderness toward the ill and disfigured, through his surprise acts of charity and hospitality to the homeless and refugees, and through his words of counsel and kindness to the world. The quote categories in this book demonstrate how Pope Francis advises us to live out that compassion through the corporal and spiritual works of mercy, through prayer, through forgiveness, through solidarity, through charity and service, through hospitality, and through a relationship with Jesus that inspires us to consecrate our hearts to Him, and then to 'draw life from His forgiveness in order to pour it out with compassion on our brothers and sisters.'

Underlying all this is Pope Francis' teaching that if we accept the mercy of God through reconciliation with Him, we will experience a transfiguration of the self that makes it possible for us to be merciful to others. 'Merciful like the Father' (*Luke* 6:36) is the motto of the Extraordinary Jubilee of Mercy that Pope Francis has established between the Feast of the Immaculate Conception on December 8, 2015, and the Feast of Christ the King on November 20, 2016. It is a period of time devoted to deepening our understanding of mercy through prayer, penance, and pardon in imitation of the merciful Father. It is a year during which Holy Doors will be opened for pilgrims in Rome and in every diocese in the world, doors that Pope Francis has called 'Gates of Mercy.'

As I conclude this writing, Pope Francis has just delivered another catechesis on the year of mercy, urging pilgrims to enter the Holy Doors seeking to receive mercy, and then to exit the doors seeking to give mercy.

'We approach that Door bringing with us our entire past, its joys and sorrows, trusting that Jesus will grant us a new beginning and revive our hope in His promises…The Church has become our mother and we are called to be witnesses of God's merciful love before the world. During this Jubilee Year, may we turn once more to Jesus, for He is the Door leading to salvation and new life. May the divine mercy which we have received pass from our hearts to our hands, and find expression in our practice of the corporal and spiritual works of mercy.'

This little book can serve as our companion on the journey of mercy, as we seek to carry these words of Pope Francis off the page and into our daily lives.

'Mercy, both in Jesus and in us, is a journey that starts from the heart to get to the hands. What does this mean? Jesus looks at you, heals you with His mercy, tells you: "Get up!" And your heart is new.'

Andrea Kirk Assaf
August 6, 2016 AD in the Year of the Extraordinary Jubilee of Mercy
Remus, Michigan

PART ONE

Compassion through Mercy

'He had compassion,' that is, His heart, His emotions, were moved! … 'Compassion' is an essential characteristic of God's mercy. God has compassion on us. What does this mean? He suffers with us, He feels our suffering. Compassion means 'suffer with.' The verb indicates that the physique is moved and trembles at the sight of the evil of man.

Mercy does not just imply being a 'good person' nor is it mere sentimentality. It is the measure of our authenticity as disciples of Jesus, and of our credibility as Christians in today's world.

We must ask the Lord to give us the grace to be merciful to those who do us wrong.

Jesus on the cross prayed for those who had crucified Him: 'Father, forgive them, they know not what they do' (*Lk* 23:34). Mercy is the only way to overcome evil. Justice is necessary, very much so, but by itself it is not enough. Justice and mercy must go together. How I wish that we could join together in a chorus of prayer, from the depths of our hearts, to implore the Lord to have mercy on us and on the whole world!

Whoever welcomes Jesus, learns to love as Jesus does. So He asks us if we want a full life: Do you want a complete life? Start by letting yourself be open and attentive! Because happiness is sown and blossoms in mercy. That is His answer, His offer, His challenge, His adventure: mercy.

God's mercy transforms human hearts; it enables us, through the experience of a faithful love, to become merciful in turn. In an ever new miracle, divine mercy shines forth in our lives, inspiring each of us to love our neighbor and to devote ourselves to what the Church's tradition calls the spiritual and corporal works of mercy. These works remind us that faith finds expression in concrete everyday actions meant to help our neighbors in body and spirit: by feeding, visiting, comforting, and instructing them. On such things will we be judged. For this reason, I expressed my hope that the Christian people may reflect on the corporal and spiritual works of mercy; this will be a way to reawaken our conscience, too often grown dull in the face of poverty, and to enter more deeply into the heart of the Gospel where the poor have a special experience of God's mercy.

Let us all ask the Lord: *'Fac cor nostrum secundum cor tuum'*: *Make our hearts like yours* (Litany of the Sacred Heart of Jesus). In this way we will receive a heart which is firm and merciful, attentive and generous, a heart which is not closed, indifferent, or prey to the globalization of indifference.

It might be said that the Gospel, the living book of God's mercy that must be continually read and reread, still has many blank pages left. It remains an open book that we are called to write in the same style, by the works of mercy we practice.

Launch us on the adventure of mercy!
Launch us on the adventure of building
bridges and tearing down walls, barriers and
barbed wire. Launch us on the adventure of
helping the poor, those who feel lonely and
abandoned, or no longer find meaning in their
lives. Send us, like Mary of Bethany, to listen
attentively to those we do not understand,
those of other cultures and peoples, even those
we are afraid of because we consider them
a threat. Make us attentive to our elders, as
Mary of Nazareth was to Elizabeth, in order
to learn from their wisdom.

People may laugh at you because you believe in the gentle and unassuming power of mercy. But do not be afraid. Think of the motto of these days: 'Blessed are the merciful, for they will receive mercy' (*Mt* 5:7).

Knowing your enthusiasm for mission, I repeat: mercy always has a youthful face! Because a merciful heart is motivated to move beyond its comfort zone. A merciful heart can go out and meet others; it is ready to embrace everyone. A merciful heart is able to be a place of refuge for those who are without a home or have lost their home; it is able to build a home and a family for those forced to emigrate; it knows the meaning of tenderness and compassion. A merciful heart can share its bread with the hungry and welcome refugees and migrants. To say the word 'mercy' along with you is to speak of opportunity, future, commitment, trust, openness, hospitality, compassion, and dreams.

Mercy, which always rejects wickedness, takes the human person in great earnest. Mercy always appeals to the goodness of each person, even though it be dormant and numbed. Far from bringing destruction, as we so often desire or want to bring about ourselves, mercy seeks to transform each situation from within. Herein lies the mystery of divine mercy. It seeks and invites us to conversion, it invites us to repentance; it invites us to see the damage being done at every level. Mercy always pierces evil in order to transform it. It is the mystery of God our Father: He sends His Son who pierced into what was evil, He took on sin in order to transform evil. This is His mercy.

The mystery of divine mercy is revealed in the history of the covenant between God and His people Israel. God shows Himself ever rich in mercy, ever ready to treat His people with deep tenderness and compassion, especially at those tragic moments when infidelity ruptures the bond of the covenant, which then needs to be ratified more firmly in justice and truth. Here is a true love story, in which God plays the role of the betrayed father and husband, while Israel plays the unfaithful child and bride. These domestic images—as in the case of Hosea (cf. *Hos* 12)—show to what extent God wishes to bind Himself to His people.

Mercy is the heart of God. It must also be the heart of the members of the one great family of His children: a heart which beats all the more strongly wherever human dignity—as a reflection of the face of God in His creatures—is in play.

The love of God breaks through that fatal withdrawal into ourselves which is indifference. The Church offers us this love of God by her teaching and especially by her witness. But we can only bear witness to what we ourselves have experienced. Christians are those who let God clothe them with goodness and mercy, with Christ, so as to become, like Christ, servants of God and others.

With the present Jubilee of Mercy I want to invite the Church to pray and work so that every Christian will have a humble and compassionate heart, one capable of proclaiming and witnessing to mercy. It is my hope that all of us will learn to 'forgive and give,' to become more open 'to those living on the outermost fringes of society, fringes which modern society itself creates,' and to refuse to fall into 'a humiliating indifference or a monotonous routine which prevents us from discovering what is new.'

God's justice is His mercy given to everyone as a grace that flows from the death and resurrection of Jesus Christ. Thus the Cross of Christ is God's judgement on all of us and on the whole world, because through it He offers us the certitude of love and new life.

The Jubilee challenges us to ... openness, and demands that we not neglect the spirit which emerged from Vatican II, the spirit of the Samaritan, as Blessed Paul VI expressed it at the conclusion of the Council. May our passing through the Holy Door today commit us to making our own the mercy of the Good Samaritan.

May the Blessed Virgin, first fruit of the saved, model of the Church, Holy and Immaculate Spouse, loved by the Lord, help us to ever increasingly rediscover divine mercy as the distinguishing mark of Christians. One cannot understand a true Christian who is not merciful, just as one cannot comprehend God without His mercy. This is the epitomizing word of the Gospel: mercy. It is the fundamental feature of the face of Christ: that face that we recognize in the various aspects of His existence: when He goes to meet everyone, when He heals the sick, when He sits at the table with sinners, and above all when, nailed to the cross, He forgives there we see the face of divine mercy.

In the present day, as the Church is charged with the task of the new evangelization, the theme of mercy needs to be proposed again and again with new enthusiasm and renewed pastoral action. It is absolutely essential for the Church and for the credibility of her message that she herself live and testify to mercy.

In short, we are called to show mercy because mercy has first been shown to us. Pardoning offences becomes the clearest expression of merciful love, and for us Christians it is an imperative from which we cannot excuse ourselves.

God's mercy has entered the heart, revealing and showing wherein our certainty and hope lie: there is always the possibility of change, we still have time to transform what is destroying us as a people, what is demeaning our humanity.

Mercy encourages us to look to the present, and to trust what is healthy and good beating in every heart. God's mercy is our shield and our strength.

The Old Testament uses various terms when it speaks about mercy. The most meaningful of these are *hesed* and *rahamim*. The first, when applied to God, expresses God's unfailing fidelity to the Covenant with His people whom He loves and forgives for ever. The second, *rahamim* ... can be translated as 'heartfelt mercy.' This particularly brings to mind the maternal womb and helps us understand that God's love for His people is like that of a mother for her child ... Love of this kind involves making space for others within ourselves and being able to sympathize, suffer and rejoice with our neighbors.

Mercy means carrying the burden of a brother or sister and helping them walk. Do not say 'ah, no, go on, go!', nor be rigid. This is very important. And who can do this? The confessor who prays, the confessor who weeps, the confessor who knows that he is more a sinner than the penitent, and if he himself has never done the bad thing that the penitent speaks of, it is but for the grace of God. Merciful is being close and accompanying the process of conversion.

Mercy is that love which embraces the misery of the human person.

We need constantly to contemplate the mystery of mercy. It is a wellspring of joy, serenity, and peace. Our salvation depends on it. Mercy: the word reveals the very mystery of the Most Holy Trinity. Mercy: the ultimate and supreme act by which God comes to meet us. Mercy: the fundamental law that dwells in the heart of every person who looks sincerely into the eyes of His brothers and sisters on the path of life. Mercy: the bridge that connects God and man, opening our hearts to the hope of being loved forever despite our sinfulness.

A little bit of mercy makes the world less cold and more just.

The mercy of God is His loving concern for each one of us. He feels responsible; that is, He desires our well-being and He wants to see us happy, full of joy, and peaceful. This is the path which the merciful love of Christians must also travel. As the Father loves, so do His children. Just as He is merciful, so we are called to be merciful to each other.

Today, more than in the past, the Gospel of mercy troubles our consciences, prevents us from taking the suffering of others for granted, and points out ways of responding which, grounded in the theological virtues of faith, hope, and charity, find practical expression in works of spiritual and corporal mercy.

People will try to block you, to make you think that God is distant, rigid, and insensitive, good to the good and bad to the bad. Instead, our heavenly Father 'makes His sun rise on the evil and on the good' (*Mt 5:45*).

To repeat continually 'for His mercy endures forever,' as the psalm does, seems to break through the dimensions of space and time, inserting everything into the eternal mystery of love. It is as if to say that not only in history, but for all eternity man will always be under the merciful gaze of the Father.

When we judge we put ourselves in God's place. This is true, but our judgment is a poor judgment: it can never, never be a true judgment because true judgment is what God gives. Why can't our judgment be like that of God? Is it because God is omnipotent and we are not? No, because our judgement lacks mercy. And when God judges, He judges with mercy.

Mercy overcomes every wall, every barrier, and leads you to always seek the face of the man, of the person. And it is mercy which changes the heart and the life, which can regenerate a person and allow him or her to integrate into society in a new way. But we know one thing: nothing is impossible for God's mercy! Even the most tangled knots are loosened by grace.

Dear brothers and sisters, the Lord never tires of having mercy on us, and wants to offer us His forgiveness once again—we all need it—inviting us to return to Him with a new heart, purified of evil, purified by tears, to take part in His joy.

In the first place, mercy is a gift of God the Father who is revealed in the Son. God's mercy gives rise to joyful gratitude for the hope which opens up before us in the mystery of our redemption by Christ's blood. Mercy nourishes and strengthens solidarity toward others as a necessary response to God's gracious love, 'which has been poured into our hearts through the Holy Spirit' (*Rom* 5:5).

With our eyes fixed on Jesus and His merciful gaze, we experience the love of the Most Holy Trinity ... His person is nothing but love, a love given gratuitously. The relationships He forms with the people who approach Him manifest something entirely unique and unrepeatable. The signs He works, especially in favor of sinners, the poor, the marginalized, the sick, and the suffering, are all meant to teach mercy. Everything in Him speaks of mercy. Nothing in Him is devoid of compassion.

We need to go forth from our own communities and be bold enough to go to the existential outskirts that need to feel the closeness of God. He abandons no one, and He always shows His unfailing tenderness and mercy, this, therefore, is what we need to take to all people.

Mercy is the true power that can save humanity and the world from sin and evil. In the Cross we see the monstrosity of man, when he allows evil to guide him but we also see the immensity of the mercy of God, who does not treat us according to our sins but according to His mercy.

The salvation which God offers us is the work of His mercy. No human efforts, however good they may be, can enable us to merit so great a gift. God, by His sheer grace, draws us to Himself and makes us one with Him. He sends His Spirit into our hearts to make us His children, transforming us and enabling us to respond to His love by our lives.

As Jesus told Saint Faustina, He is happy when we tell Him everything: He is not bored with our lives, which He already knows, He waits for us to tell Him even about the events of our day (cf. *Diary*, 6 September 1937). That is the way to seek God: through prayer that is transparent and unafraid to hand over to Him our troubles, our struggles and our resistance. Jesus' heart is won over by sincere openness, by hearts capable of acknowledging and grieving over their weakness, yet trusting that precisely there God's mercy will be active.

In the corporal works of mercy we touch the flesh of Christ in our brothers and sisters who need to be fed, clothed, sheltered, visited in the spiritual works of mercy—counsel, instruction, forgiveness, admonishment, and prayer—we touch more directly our own sinfulness. The corporal and spiritual works of mercy must never be separated. By touching the flesh of the crucified Jesus in the suffering, sinners can receive the gift of realizing that they too are poor and in need. By taking this path, the 'proud,' the 'powerful,' and the 'wealthy' spoken of in the *Magnificat* can also be embraced and undeservedly loved by the crucified Lord who died and rose for them. This love alone is the answer to that yearning for infinite happiness and love that we think we can satisfy with the idols of knowledge, power, and riches.

PART TWO:

*Compassion
through Prayer*

A prayer that does not lead you to practical action for your brother—the poor, the sick, those in need of help, a brother in difficulty—is a sterile and incomplete prayer. But, in the same way ... When time is not set aside for dialogue with Him in prayer, we risk serving ourselves and not God present in our needy brother and sister.

The prayers of the Church on earth
establish a communion of mutual service
and goodness which reaches up into the sight
of God. Together with the saints who have
found their fulfilment in God, we form part
of that communion in which indifference
is conquered by love. The Church in heaven
is not triumphant because she has turned
her back on the sufferings of the world and
rejoices in splendid isolation. Rather, the
saints already joyfully contemplate the fact
that, through Jesus' death and resurrection,
they have triumphed once and for all over

indifference, hardness of heart, and hatred. Until this victory of love penetrates the whole world, the saints continue to accompany us on our pilgrim way. Saint Thérèse of Lisieux, a Doctor of the Church, expressed her conviction that the joy in heaven for the victory of crucified love remains incomplete as long as there is still a single man or woman on earth who suffers and cries out in pain: 'I trust fully that I shall not remain idle in heaven, my desire is to continue to work for the Church and for souls' (*Letter* 254, July 14, 1897).

St Benedict sums up the kind of life that indicated for his monks in two words: *ora et labora*, pray and work. It is from contemplation, from a strong friendship with the Lord that the capacity is born in us to live and to bring the love of God, His mercy, His tenderness, to others. And also our work with brothers in need, our charitable works of mercy, lead us to the Lord, because it is in the needy brother and sister that we see the Lord Himself.

We celebrate the fact that coming from different cultures, we have come together to pray. Let our best word, our best argument, be our unity in prayer. Let us take a moment of silence and pray. Let us place before the Lord these testimonies of our friends, and let us identify with those for whom 'the family is a meaningless concept, the home only a place to sleep and eat,' and with those who live with the fear that their mistakes and sins have made them outcasts. Let us also place before the Lord your own 'battles,' the interior struggles that each of you carries in his or her heart.

Entrusting ourselves to God's will in fact means remitting ourselves to His infinite mercy. I will even share with you a personal confidence. In the evening, before going to bed, I say this short prayer: 'Lord, if you will, you can make me clean!' And I pray five 'Our Fathers,' one for each of Jesus' wounds, because Jesus has cleansed us with His wounds. If I do this, you can do it too, in your home, and say: 'Lord, if you will, you can make me clean!', and think about Jesus' wounds and say an 'Our Father' for each of them. Jesus always hears us.

In a world which all too often is merciless to the sinner and lenient to the sin, we need to cultivate a strong sense of justice, to discern and to do God's will. Amid a culture of indifference which not infrequently turns ruthless, our style of life should instead be devout, filled with empathy, compassion, and mercy, drawn daily from the wellspring of prayer.

Prayer is the strength of the Christian and of every person who believes. In the weakness and frailty of our lives, we can turn to God with the confidence of children and enter into communion with Him. In the face of so many wounds that hurt us and could harden our hearts, we are called to dive into the sea of prayer, which is the sea of God's boundless love, to taste His tenderness.

We all have our likes and dislikes, and perhaps at this very moment we are angry with someone. At least let us say to the Lord, 'Lord, I am angry with this person, with that person. I pray to you for him and for her.' To pray for a person with whom I am irritated is a beautiful step forward in love, and an act of evangelization.

This is what prayer does: it transforms the desire and models it according to the will of God, whatever that may be, because the one who prays aspires first of all to union with God, who is merciful Love.

All families, we need God: all of us! We need His help, His strength, His mercy, His forgiveness. And we need simplicity to pray as a family: simplicity is necessary! Praying the Our Father together, around the table, is not something extraordinary: it's easy. And praying the Rosary together, as a family, is very beautiful and a source of great strength! And also praying for one another! The husband for his wife, the wife for her husband, both together for their children, the children for their grandparents … praying for each other. This is what it means to pray in the family, and it is what makes the family strong: prayer.

Do I pray for my enemies or do I wish something bad for them? … Who are my enemies, who has hurt me, who is it that I don't love or who am I distanced from? Who are they? Do I pray for them? … May the Lord give us the grace to pray for our enemies, to pray for those who wish us ill, who do not love us, to pray for those who do us harm, who persecute us …We will see that this prayer will bear two fruits: it will improve our enemy, because prayer is powerful and it will make us more as children of the Father.

You can do so many things, so many works, even works of mercy, you can do many great things for the Church—a Catholic university, a college, a hospital—and they might even build a monument to you as a benefactor of the Church, but if you do not pray, none of this will bring light. How many works become dark due to a lack of light, a lack of prayer? Prayer of adoration to the Father, of praise to the Trinity, the prayer of thanksgiving, even prayer to ask things of the Lord ... must always be a heartfelt prayer. This is the oil, it is the battery, which gives life to the light.

You pray for the hungry. Then you feed them. That's how prayer works.

'Be merciful just as your Father is merciful' (*Lk* 6:36). It is a programme of life as demanding as it is rich with joy and peace. Jesus's command is directed to anyone willing to listen to His voice (cf. *Lk* 6:27). In order to be capable of mercy, therefore, we must first of all dispose ourselves to listen to the Word of God. This means rediscovering the value of silence in order to meditate on the Word that comes to us. In this way, it will be possible to contemplate God's mercy and adopt it as our lifestyle.

It is not enough, therefore, to ask *how much* we pray, we have to ask ourselves *how we* pray, or better, in *what state our heart is*: it is important to examine it so as to evaluate our thoughts, our feelings, and root out arrogance and hypocrisy. But, I ask myself: can one pray with arrogance? No. Can one pray with hypocrisy? No. We must only pray by placing ourselves before God just as we are ... We are all taken up by the frenetic pace of daily life, often at the mercy of feelings, dazed and confused. It is necessary to learn how to rediscover the path to our heart, to recover the value of intimacy and silence, because the God who encounters us and speaks to us is there. Only by beginning there can we in our turn encounter others and speak with them.

What a beautiful thing that the Church begins her daily prayer with the words, 'O God, come to my assistance. O Lord, make haste to help me' (*Ps* 70:2)! The assistance we ask for is already the first step of God's mercy toward us. He comes to assist us in our weakness. And His help consists in helping us accept His presence and closeness to us. Day after day, touched by His compassion, we also can become compassionate toward others.

Prayer enables grace to open a way out from closure to openness, from fear to courage, from sadness to joy ... *from division to unity.*

Humility is the necessary condition to be raised by Him, so as to experience the mercy that comes to fill our emptiness. If the prayer of the proud does not reach God's heart, the humility of the poor opens it wide.

We ask the Lord for a faith which becomes unceasing prayer ... a faith that is nourished by the desire of His arrival. And in this prayer we experience the compassion of God, like a Father who comes to meet His children full of merciful love.

The primary reason for evangelizing is the love of Jesus which we have received, the experience of salvation which urges us to ever greater love of Him. What kind of love would not feel the need to speak of the beloved, to point Him out, to make Him known? If we do not feel an intense desire to share this love, we need to pray insistently that He will once more touch our hearts. We need to implore His grace daily, asking Him to open our cold hearts and shake up our lukewarm and superficial existence.

May each family rediscover family prayer, which helps to bring about mutual understanding and forgiveness.

How good it is to stand before a crucifix, or on our knees before the Blessed Sacrament, and simply to be in His presence! How much good it does us when He once more touches our lives and impels us to share His new life!

Let us peer for a moment into the heart of Saint Paul, to see what his prayer was like. It was full of people: '... I constantly pray with you in every one of my prayers for all of you ... because I hold you in my heart' (*Phil* 1:4, 7). Here we see that intercessory prayer does not divert us from true contemplation, since authentic contemplation always has a place for others.

When evangelizers rise from prayer, their hearts are more open, freed of self-absorption, they are desirous of doing good and sharing their lives with others.

Prayer, humility, and charity toward all are essential in the Christian life: they are the way to holiness.

Breathing is made up of two stages: inhaling, the intake of air, and exhaling, the letting out of air. The spiritual life is fed, nourished, by prayer and is expressed outwardly through mission: inhaling and exhaling. When we inhale, by prayer, we receive the fresh air of the Holy Spirit.

We all have our likes and dislikes, and perhaps at this very moment we are angry with someone. At least let us say to the Lord: 'Lord, I am angry with this person, with that person. I pray to you for him or for her.' To pray for a person with whom I am irritated is a beautiful step forward in love, and an act of evangelization.

In these difficult moments it is necessary to trust in God's help through childlike prayer, and, at the same time, it is important to find the courage and the humility to open up to others, to ask for help, to ask for a helping hand. How often have we done this and then succeeded in emerging from our difficulty and finding God again! In this communion ... we form a great family, where every member is helped and sustained by the others.

PART THREE:

Compassion through Forgiveness

What does Jesus ask of us? He desires hearts that are truly consecrated, hearts that draw life from His forgiveness in order to pour it out with compassion on our brothers and sisters.

One of the most obvious works of mercy, and perhaps the most difficult to put into practice, is to forgive those who have offended us, who have done us wrong or whom we consider to be enemies. 'At times how hard it seems to forgive! And yet pardon is the instrument placed into our fragile hands to attain serenity of heart. To let go of anger, wrath, violence, and revenge are necessary conditions to living joyfully' (*Misericordiae Vultus*, 9).

Jesus tells us: 'Blessed are the merciful, for they shall find mercy' (*Mt* 5:7). Blessed indeed are they who can forgive, who show heartfelt compassion, who are capable of offering the very best of themselves to others.

Let us ask the Lord to teach us, first, to leave all rigidity, but to go upwards, to be able to adore and praise God that He may teach us to be reconciled with one another and also, that He may teach us to agree with each other to the extent that we can.

Despite the child's wrong attitude that deserves punishment, a father's love is faithful. He always forgives his repentant children. We see here how forgiveness is always included in mercy. It is 'not an abstract idea, but a concrete reality with which he reveals his love as that of a father or a mother, moved to the very depths out of love for their child … It gushes forth from the depths naturally, full of tenderness and compassion, indulgence and mercy' (*Misericordiae Vultus*, 6).

A person unable to forgive has not yet known the fullness of love. Only one who truly loves is able to forgive and forget.

We keep looking for God, but God is there before us, always looking for us, and He finds us first. Maybe one of you feels something weighing on your heart. You are thinking: I did this, I did that ... Do not be afraid! God is waiting for you! God is a Father and He is always waiting for us! It is so wonderful to feel the merciful embrace of the Father in the sacrament of Reconciliation, to discover that the confessional is a place of mercy, and to allow ourselves to be touched by the merciful love of the Lord who always forgives us!

Situations can change, people can change. Be the first to seek to bring good. Do not grow accustomed to evil, but defeat it with good.

Even if the life of a person has been a disaster, even if it is destroyed by vices, drugs, or anything else—God is in this person's life. You can, you must try to seek God in every human life. Although the life of a person is a land full of thorns and weeds, there is always a space in which the good seed can grow. You have to trust God.

Trust the memory of God: His memory is not a 'hard disk' that 'saves' and 'archives' all our data, but a heart filled with tender compassion, one that finds joy in 'erasing' in us every trace of evil.

Dear young friends, don't be ashamed to bring everything to the Lord in confession, especially your weaknesses, your struggles and your sins. He will surprise you with His forgiveness and His peace. Don't be afraid to say 'yes' to Him with all your heart, to respond generously and to follow Him! Don't let your soul grow numb, but aim for the goal of a beautiful love which also demands sacrifice. Say a firm 'no' to the narcotic of success at any cost and the sedative of worrying only about yourself and your own comfort.

The Lord asks us above all *not to judge* and *not to condemn.* If anyone wishes to avoid God's judgement, He should not make himself the judge of his brother or sister. Human beings, whenever they judge, look no farther than the surface, whereas the Father looks into the very depths of the soul. How much harm words do when they are motivated by feelings of jealousy and envy! To speak ill of others puts them in a bad light, undermines their reputation and leaves them prey to the whims of gossip. To refrain from judgement and condemnation means, in a positive sense, to know how to accept the good in every person and to spare him any suffering that might be caused by our partial judgment, our presumption to know everything about him.

In Jesus crucified, God shows His desire to draw near to sinners, however far they may have strayed from Him.

It is possible to create something new within ourselves and around us, simply because God is faithful, always faithful, for He cannot deny Himself, He continues to be rich in goodness and mercy, and He is always ready to forgive and start afresh.

God is waiting for you. And if you were a great sinner, He is waiting for you even more and waiting for you with great love ...

If God limited Himself to only justice, He would cease to be God, and would instead be like human beings who ask merely that the law be respected. But mere justice is not enough. Experience shows that an appeal to justice alone will result in its destruction. This is why God goes beyond justice with His mercy and forgiveness.

In the Year of Mercy, every Christian family can become a privileged place on this pilgrimage for experiencing the joy of forgiveness: forgiveness is the essence of the love which can understand mistakes and mend them—how miserable we would be if God did not forgive us. Within the family we learn how to forgive, because we are certain that we are understood and supported, whatever the mistakes we make. Let us not lose confidence in the family!

It is beautiful when we can always open our hearts to one another, and hide nothing. Where there is love, there is also understanding and forgiveness. To all of you, dear families, I entrust this most important mission, the domestic pilgrimage of daily family life which the world and the Church need, now more than ever.

The family, where we keep loving one another despite our limits and sins ... becomes a school of forgiveness.

We are all sinners, but we are all forgiven: we all have the possibility of receiving this pardon, which is the mercy of God. We need not fear, therefore, to recognize ourselves sinners, confess ourselves sinners, because every sin was carried by the Son to the Cross.

May our way of communicating help to overcome the mindset that neatly separates sinners from the righteous. We can and we must judge situations of sin—such as violence, corruption, and exploitation—but we may not judge individuals, since only God can see into the depths of their hearts.

Pardoning offences becomes the clearest expression of merciful love, and for us Christians it is an imperative from which we cannot excuse ourselves. At times how hard it seems to forgive! And yet pardon is the instrument placed into our fragile hands to attain serenity of heart.

To let go of anger, wrath, violence, and revenge are necessary conditions to living joyfully. Let us therefore heed the Apostle's exhortation: 'Do not let the sun go down on your anger' (*Eph* 4:26).

Only one who has been caressed by the tenderness of mercy truly knows the Lord. The privileged place of encounter is the caress of Jesus' mercy regarding my sin. This is why you may have heard me say, several times, that the place for this, the privileged place of the encounter with Jesus Christ is my sin. The will to respond and to change, which can give rise to a different life, comes thanks to this merciful embrace.

In life we err frequently, we make many mistakes ... We accuse the other to avoid saying 'I'm sorry,' or 'Forgive me.' It's an old story! It is an instinct that stands at the origin of so many disasters.

How good it feels to come back to Him whenever we are lost! Let me say this once more: God never tires of forgiving us, we are the ones who tire of seeking His mercy.

Christ, who told us to forgive one another 'seventy times seven' (*Mt* 18:22) has given us His example: He has forgiven us seventy times seven. Time and time again He bears us on His shoulders. No one can strip us of the dignity bestowed upon us by this boundless and unfailing love. With a tenderness which never disappoints, but is always capable of restoring our joy, He makes it possible for us to lift up our heads and to start anew. Let us not flee from the resurrection of Jesus, let us never give up, come what will. May nothing inspire more than His life, which impels us onward!

May the message of mercy reach everyone, and may no one be indifferent to the call to experience mercy. I direct this invitation to conversion even more fervently to those whose behaviour distances them from the grace of God … For their own good, I beg them to change their lives.

God's forgiveness knows no bounds. In the death and resurrection of Jesus Christ, God makes even more evident His love and its power to destroy all human sin ...

Our infinite sadness can only be cured by an infinite love.

In the Sacrament of Reconciliation, God forgives our sins, which He truly blots out and yet sin leaves a negative effect on the way we think and act. But the mercy of God is stronger even than this. It … reaches the pardoned sinner and frees him from every residue left by the consequences of sin, enabling him to act with charity, to grow in love rather than to fall back into sin.

To weep over injustice, to cry over corruption, to cry over oppression. These are tears that lead to transformation, that soften the heart they are the tears that purify our gaze and enable us to see the cycle of sin into which very often we have sunk. They are tears that can sensitize our gaze and our attitude hardened and especially dormant in the face of another's suffering. They are the tears that can break us, capable of opening us to conversion.

Going out to others in order to reach the fringes of humanity does not mean rushing out aimlessly into the world. Often it is better simply to slow down, to put aside our eagerness in order to see and listen to others, to stop rushing from one thing to another and to remain with someone who has faltered along the way. At times we have to be like the father of the prodigal son, who always keeps his door open so that when the son returns, he can readily pass through it.

Only words spoken with love and accompanied by meekness and mercy can touch our sinful hearts. Harsh and moralistic words and actions risk further alienating those whom we wish to lead to conversion and freedom, reinforcing their sense of rejection and defensiveness.

God is always ready to forgive, and He never tires of forgiving in ways that are continually new and surprising.

Decisive is the *compassionate gaze* of the Lord after Peter had denied Him three times: a gaze that pierces the heart and brings tears of repentance (cf. *Lk* 22:61–62). At that moment, Simon Peter *was set free from the prison of his selfish pride and fear,* and overcame the temptation of closing his heart to Jesus's call to follow Him along the way of the cross.

PART FOUR:

The compassion of God, His suffering with us, gives meaning and worth to our struggles and suffering.

We are called not only to respect the natural environment, but also to show respect for, and solidarity with, all the members of our human family. These two dimensions are closely related today; we are suffering from a crisis which is not only about the just management of economic resources, but also about concern for human resources, for the needs of our brothers and sisters living in extreme poverty, and especially for the many children in our world lacking adequate education, healthcare, and nutrition. Consumerism and a 'culture of waste' have led some of us to tolerate the waste of precious resources, including food, while others are literally wasting away from hunger. I ask all of you to reflect on this grave ethical problem in a spirit of solidarity grounded in our common responsibility for the earth and for all our brothers and sisters in the human family.

It is necessary today, more than ever, to educate ourselves in solidarity, rediscovering the value and meaning of this uncomfortable word which is so often set aside, and to turn it into the attitude that forms the basis of decisions made at a political, economic, and financial level, and of relations between people, populations, and nations.

Solidarity represents the moral and social attitude which best corresponds to an awareness of the scourges of our own day, and to the growing interdependence, especially in a globalized world, between the lives of given individuals and communities and those of other men and women in the rest of the world.

We too, then, are called to make compassion, love, mercy, and solidarity a true way of life, a rule of conduct in our relationships with one another. This requires the conversion of our hearts: the grace of God has to turn our hearts of stone into hearts of flesh (cf. *Ezek* 36:26), open to others in authentic solidarity. For solidarity is much more than a 'feeling of vague compassion or shallow distress at the misfortunes of so many people, both near and far.' Solidarity is 'a firm and persevering determination to commit oneself to the common good, that is to say to the good of all and of each individual, because we are all really responsible for all,' because compassion flows from fraternity.

You tell us that to love God and your neighbor is not something abstract, but profoundly concrete: it means seeing in every person the face of the Lord to be served, to serve Him concretely. And you are, dear brothers and sisters, the face of Jesus.

When we live out a spirituality of drawing nearer to others and seeking their welfare, our hearts are opened wide to the Lord's greatest and most beautiful gifts. Whenever we encounter another person in love, we learn something new about God. Whenever our eyes are opened to acknowledge the other, we grow in the light of faith and knowledge of God.

We know how much violence has resulted in recent times from the attempt to eliminate God and the divine from the horizon of humanity, and we are aware of the importance of witnessing in our societies that primordial openness to transcendence which lies deep within the human heart. In this, we also sense our closeness to all those men and women who, although not identifying themselves as followers of any religious tradition, are nonetheless searching for truth, goodness, and beauty; the truth, goodness, and beauty of God. They are our valued allies in the commitment to defending human dignity, in building a peaceful coexistence between peoples and in safeguarding and caring for creation.

We achieve fulfilment when we break down walls and our heart is filled with faces and names!

There are many good reasons to believe in mankind's capacity to act together in solidarity and, on the basis of our interconnection and interdependence, to demonstrate concern for the more vulnerable of our brothers and sisters and for the protection of the common good. This attitude of mutual responsibility is rooted in our fundamental vocation to fraternity and a life in common.

Personal dignity and interpersonal relationships are what constitute us as human beings whom God willed to create in His own image and likeness. As creatures endowed with inalienable dignity, we are related to all our brothers and sisters, for whom we are responsible and with whom we act in solidarity. Lacking this relationship, we would be less human. We see, then, how indifference represents a menace to the human family.

As we continue our earthly pilgrimage, if we learn to bear each other's burdens and to exchange the rich patrimony of our respective traditions, then we will see more clearly that what unites us is greater than what divides us.

Sadly, war and terrorism, accompanied by kidnapping, ethnic or religious persecution, and the misuse of power, marked the past year from start to finish ... Yet some events of the year now ending inspire me, in looking ahead to the new year, to encourage everyone not to lose hope in our human ability to conquer evil and to combat resignation and indifference. They demonstrate our capacity to show solidarity and to rise above self-interest, apathy, and indifference in the face of critical situations.

Our words and actions should be such as to help us all escape the vicious circles of condemnation and vengeance which continue to ensnare individuals and nations, encouraging expressions of hatred. The words of Christians ought to be a constant encouragement to communion and, even in those cases where they must firmly condemn evil, they should never try to rupture relationships and communication.

The example of the martyrs also teaches us the importance of charity in the life of faith. It was the purity of their witness to Christ, expressed in an acceptance of the equal dignity of all the baptized, which led them to a form of fraternal life that challenged the rigid social structures of their day. It was their refusal to separate the twin commandment of love of God and love of neighbor which impelled them to such great solicitude for the needs of the brethren. Their example has much to say to us who live in societies where, alongside immense wealth, dire poverty is silently growing where the cry of the poor is seldom heeded and where Christ continues to call out to us, asking us to love and serve Him by tending to our brothers and sisters in need.

Sometimes we are tempted to be that kind of Christian who keeps the Lord's wounds at arm's length. Yet Jesus wants us to touch human misery, to touch the suffering flesh of others ... Wherever we do so, our lives become wonderfully complicated and we experience intensely what it is to be a people, to be part of a people.

As Christians we are called to strengthen the fraternal communion among us, so as to bear witness to the Gospel of Christ and to be a leaven of a more just and united society.

You willed that your ministers would also be clothed in weakness in order that they may feel compassion for those in ignorance and error: let everyone who approaches them feel sought after, loved, and forgiven by God.

History teaches us that the path of peace requires great tenacity and continuous steps, starting with small steps and gradually increasing them, going to meet one another. Precisely for this reason my hope is that each and every person may give his or her own contribution to peace and reconciliation.

It is not a question of a mission reserved only to a few: 'The Church, guided by the Gospel of mercy and by love for mankind, hears the cry for justice and intends to respond to it with all her might.' In this context we can understand Jesus' command to His disciples: 'You yourselves give them something to eat!' (*Mk* 6:37): it means working to eliminate the structural causes of poverty and to promote the integral development of the poor, as well as small daily acts of solidarity in meeting the real needs which we encounter.

Human dignity is the same for all human beings: when we trample on the dignity of another, I am trampling on my own.

We must recover the whole sense of gift, of gratuitousness, of solidarity. Rampant capitalism has taught the logic of profit at all costs, of giving to get, of exploitation without looking at the person … and we are seeing the results in the crisis we are experiencing!

With a contemplative gaze, a gaze of faith which sees God dwelling in their homes, in their streets and squares ... He dwells among them, fostering solidarity, fraternity, and the desire for goodness, truth, and justice. This presence must not be contrived but found, uncovered. God does not hide Himself from those who seek Him with a sincere heart.

In this Holy Year, we look forward to the experience of opening our hearts to those living on the outermost fringes of society: fringes which modern society itself creates. How many uncertain and painful situations there are in the world today! How many are the wounds borne by the flesh of those who have no voice because their cry is muffled and drowned out by the indifference of the rich! During this Jubilee, the Church will be called even more to heal these wounds, to assuage them with the oil of consolation, to bind them with mercy and cure them with solidarity and vigilant care. Let us not fall into humiliating indifference or a monotonous routine that prevents us from discovering what is new!

In our throwaway culture, in which what we do not need, we cast aside, leaving only those who consider themselves righteous, who feel pure, who feel clean—poor things!—this word, solidarity, risks being cancelled from the dictionary, because it is an inconvenient word, because it obliges us to look to others, and to give ourselves to others with love.

It is not just petty love that we can offer one another, but something much more profound: it is a communion that renders us able to enter into the joy and sorrow of others and make them sincerely our own.

To live as true children of God means to love our neighbor and to be close to those who are lonely and in difficulty.

Some people are well-informed, they listen to the radio, read the newspapers or watch television, but they do so mechanically and without engagement. They are vaguely aware of the tragedies afflicting humanity, but they have no sense of involvement or compassion. Theirs is the attitude of those who know, but keep their gaze, their thoughts and their actions focused on themselves. Sadly, it must be said that today's information explosion does not of itself lead to an increased concern for other people's problems, which demands openness and a sense of solidarity.

Jesus tells us that love for others—
foreigners, the sick, prisoners, the
homeless, even our enemies—is the yardstick
by which God will judge our actions. Our
eternal destiny depends on this. It is not
surprising that the Apostle Paul tells the
Christians of Rome to rejoice with those who
rejoice and to weep with those who weep

(cf. *Rom* 12:15), or that He encourages the Corinthians to take up collections as a sign of solidarity with the suffering members of the Church (cf. *1 Cor* 16:23). And Saint John writes: 'If anyone has the world's goods and sees his brother or sister in need, yet refuses help, how does God's love abide in him?' (*1 Jn* 3:17 cf. *Jas* 2:15–16).

Do not stand by classifying others by sight who is neighbor and who is not. You can become neighbor to any needy person you meet, and you will know that you have compassion in your heart, that is, whether you have the capacity to suffer with the other.

Mercy is the heart of God. It must also be the heart of the members of the one great family of His children: a heart which beats all the more strongly wherever human dignity—as a reflection of the face of God in His creatures—is in play.

Our faith in Christ, who became poor, and was always close to the poor and the outcast, is the basis of our concern for the integral development of society's most neglected members.

Without a witness to mercy, life becomes fruitless and sterile, as if sequestered in a barren desert. The time has come for the Church to take up the joyful call to mercy once more. It is time to return to the basics and to bear the weaknesses and struggles of our brothers and sisters. Mercy is the force that reawakens us to new life and instills in us the courage to look to the future with hope.

Let us ward off destructive cynicism! Let us open our eyes and see the misery of the world, the wounds of our brothers and sisters who are denied their dignity, and let us recognize that we are compelled to heed their cry for help! May we reach out to them and support them so they can feel the warmth of our presence, our friendship, and our fraternity! May their cry become our own, and together may we break down the barriers of indifference that too often reign supreme and mask our hypocrisy and egoism!

In many places, generally speaking, due to the economic humanism that has been imposed in the world, the culture of exclusion, of rejection, is spreading. There is no place for the elderly or the unwanted child, there is no time for that unwanted person in the street. At times, it seems that for some people, human relations are regulated by two modern 'dogmas': efficiency and pragmatism ... [Have] the courage to go against the tide of this culture. Be courageous!

No one can say that they cannot be close to the poor because their own lifestyle demands more attention to other areas. This is an excuse commonly heard in academic, business, or professional, and even ecclesial, circles. While it is quite true that the essential vocation and mission of the lay faithful is to strive that earthly realities and all human activity may be transformed by the Gospel, none of us can think we are exempt for concern for the poor and for social justice.

Let us remember well, however, that whenever food is thrown out it is as if food were stolen from the table of the poor, from the hungry! I ask everyone to reflect on the loss and the waste of food, to identify ways and approaches which, by seriously dealing with this problem, convey solidarity and sharing with the underprivileged.

Paradoxically, in a moment in which globalization allows us to be informed of situations of need throughout the world, and to multiply exchanges and human relations, there appears to be a growing tendency towards individualism and inwardness, which leads to a certain attitude of indifference—at a personal, institutional, and state level—towards those who die of hunger and suffer as a result of malnutrition, as if it were an inescapable fact.

The way to relate to others which truly heals instead of debilitating us, is a mystical fraternity, a contemplative fraternity. It is a fraternal love capable of seeing the sacred grandeur of our neighbor, of finding God in every human being, of tolerating the nuisances of life in common by clinging to the love of God, of opening the heart to divine love and seeking the happiness of others just as their heavenly Father does.

To go out of ourselves and to join others is healthy for us. To be self-enclosed is to taste the bitter poison of imminence, and humanity will be worse for every selfish choice we make.

Every period of history is marked by the presence of human weakness, self-absorption, complacency, and selfishness, to say nothing of the concupiscence which preys upon us all. These things are ever present under one guise or another, they are due to our human limits rather than particular situations. Let us not say, then, that things are harder today—they are simply different. But let us learn also from the saints who have gone before us, who confronted the difficulties of their own day. So I propose that we pause to rediscover some of the reasons which can help us to imitate them today.

Today, when the networks and means of human communication have made unprecedented advances, we sense the challenge of finding and sharing a 'mystique' of living together, of mingling and encounter, of embracing and supporting one another, of stepping into this flood tide which, while chaotic, can become a genuine experience of fraternity, a caravan of solidarity, a sacred pilgrimage. Greater possibilities for communication thus turn into greater possibilities for encounter and solidarity for everyone.

The Gospel tells us constantly to run the risk of a face-to-face encounter with others, with their physical presence which challenges us, with their pain and their pleas, with their joy which infects us in our close and continuous interaction.

Be active members! Go on the offensive! Play down the field, build a better world, a world of brothers and sisters, a world of justice, of peace, of fraternity, of solidarity. Play always on the offensive!

To paraphrase Saint James, we can say that mercy without works is dead. To be merciful like God our Father demands constant sensitivity to the needs, material and spiritual, of those around us. Jesus Himself tells us in no uncertain terms that we will be judged by the mercy we show to the poor: those who hunger and thirst, the naked, the stranger, the sick and those in prison (cf. *Mt* 25:35–36). Particularly in our prosperous societies, Christians are called to guard against the temptation of indifference to the plea of so many of our brothers and sisters.

In our rapidly changing and increasingly globalized world, many new forms of poverty are appearing. In response to them, may we prove creative in developing new and practical forms of charitable outreach as an expression of the way of mercy.

How important it is that the voice of every member of society be heard, and that a spirit of open communication, dialogue and cooperation be fostered. It is likewise important that special concern be shown for the poor, the vulnerable, and those who have no voice, not only by meeting their immediate needs but also by assisting them in their human and cultural advancement.

Each of us should find ways to communicate with Jesus wherever we are. All of us are called to offer others an explicit witness to the saving love of the Lord, who despite our imperfections offers us His closeness, His word and His strength, and gives meaning to our lives. In your heart you know that it is not the same to live without Him; what you have come to realize, what has helped you to live and given you hope, is what you also need to communicate to others.

PART FIVE:

Compassion through Charity and Service

We thank God, who has raised up in many a desire to be close to their neighbor and to follow in this manner the law of charity which is the heart of the Gospel. But charity is even yet more authentic and more incisive when it is lived in communion. Communion shows that charity is not merely about helping others, but is a dimension that permeates the whole of life and breaks down all those barriers of individualism which prevent us from encountering one another. Charity is the inner life of the Church and is manifested in ecclesial communion.

The call to serve involves something special, to which we must be attentive. Serving means caring … for the vulnerable of our families, our society, our people. Theirs are the suffering, fragile, and downcast faces which Jesus tells us specifically to look at and which He asks us to love. With a love which takes shape in our actions and decisions. With a love which finds expression in whatever tasks we, as citizens, are called to perform. It is people of flesh and blood, people with individual lives and stories, and with all their frailty, that Jesus asks us to protect, to care for, and to serve. Being a Christian entails promoting the dignity of our brothers and sisters, fighting for it, living for it. That is why Christians are constantly called to set aside their own wishes and desires, their pursuit of power, before the concrete gaze of those who are most vulnerable.

These two criteria are like the pillars of true love: deeds, and the gift of self.

God's fatherly care extends to everyone, like the care of a shepherd for his flock, but it is particularly concerned for the needs of the sheep who are wounded, weary or ill. Jesus told us that the Father stoops to help those overcome by physical or moral poverty; the more serious their condition, the more powerfully is His divine mercy revealed.

To all of you, especially those who can do more and give more, I ask: Please, do more! Please, give more! When you give of your time, your talents, and your resources to the many people who struggle and who live on the margins, you make a difference. It is a difference that is so desperately needed, and one for which you will be richly rewarded by the Lord.

For us Christians, love of neighbor springs from love of God and it is its most limpid expression. Here one tries to love one's neighbor, but also to allow oneself to be loved by one's neighbor. These two attitudes go together, one cannot be exercised without the other. Printed on the letterhead of the Missionaries of Charity are these words of Jesus: 'as you did it to one of the least of these my brethren, you did it to me' (*Mt* 25:40). Loving God in our brethren and loving our brethren in God.

What counts above all else is 'faith working through love' (*Gal* 5:6). Works of love directed to one's neighbor are the most perfect external manifestation of the interior grace of the Spirit. . .

Jesus wanted to show us His heart as the heart that loved so deeply. For this reason we have this commemoration today, especially of God's love. God loved us, He loved us with such great love. I am thinking of what St Ignatius told us … He pointed out two criteria on love. The first: love is expressed more clearly in actions than in words. The second: there is greater love in giving than in receiving.

Continue to overcome apathy, offering a Christian response to the social and political anxieties, which are arising in various parts of the world. I ask you to be builders of the world, to work for a better world. Dear young people, please, don't be observers of life, but get involved. Jesus did not remain an observer, but He immersed Himself. Don't be observers, but immerse yourself in the reality of life, as Jesus did.

Faith teaches us to see that every man and woman represents a blessing for me, that the light of God's face shines on me through the faces of my brothers and sisters.

We see how faith brings light and hope in situations of grave hardship, we observe how faith is rekindled in hearts touched by the Spirit of Jesus who said, 'Whoever receives one such child in my name receives me' (*Mk* 9:37). This faith, working through charity, dislodges the mountains of indifference, of disbelief, and of apathy, and opens hands and hearts to work for what is good …

Through humble gestures and simple acts of service to the least among us, the Good News that Jesus is risen and lives among us is proclaimed.

The Extraordinary Jubilee Year of Mercy, which is before us, is a propitious occasion to work together in the field of the works of charity. In this field, where compassion counts above all else, we may be joined by many people who are not believers or who are in search of God and of the Truth, people who place at the center the face of another person, in particular the face of a needy brother or sister.

The mercy to which we are called embraces all of creation, which God entrusted to us so that we keep it, not exploit it or, worse still, destroy it. We must always seek to leave the world better than we found it (cf. *Encyclical Laudato Si',* n. 194), beginning with the environment in which we live, and the small gestures of our daily life.

To protect creation, to protect every man and every woman, to look upon them with tenderness and love, is to open up a horizon of hope. It is to let a shaft of light break through the heavy clouds. It is to bring the warmth of hope!

That is the purpose of our mission: to identify the material and immaterial needs of the people and try to meet them as we can. Do you know what *agape* is? It is love of others, as our Lord preached. It is not proselytizing, it is love. Love for one's neighbor, that leavening that serves the common good.

Accompanying on its own is not enough. It is not enough to offer someone a sandwich unless it is accompanied by the possibility of learning how to stand on one's own two feet. Charity that leaves the poor person as he is, is not sufficient. True mercy, the mercy God gives to us and teaches us, demands justice, it demands that the poor find the way to be poor no longer. It asks— and it asks us, the Church, us, the City of Rome, it asks the institutions—to ensure that no one ever again stand in need of a soup-kitchen, of makeshift lodgings, of a service of legal assistance in order to have his legitimate right recognized to live and to work, to be fully a person.

If something should rightly disturb us and trouble our consciences, it is the fact that so many of our brothers and sisters are living without the strength, light, and consolation born of friendship with Jesus Christ, without a community of faith to support them, without meaning and a goal in life. More than by fear of going astray, my hope is that

we will be moved by the fear of remaining
shut up within structures which give us a false
sense of security, within rules which make us
harsh judges, within habits which make
us feel safe, while at our door people are
starving and Jesus does not tire of saying to
us: 'Give them something to eat' (*Mk* 6:37).

Let us never forget this: before the suffering of so many people exhausted by hunger, violence, and injustice, we cannot remain spectators. What does it mean to ignore the suffering of man? It means to ignore God! If I do not draw close to that man, that woman, that child, that elderly man or woman who are suffering, I do not draw close to God.

May our Mother of Mercy teach us how to take concrete care of the wounds of Jesus in our brothers and sisters in need, those close at hand and those far away, the sick and the migrant, because by serving those who suffer we honour the flesh of Christ.

We must not forget that true power, at whatever level, is service, which has its luminous summit on the Cross.

With great wisdom Benedict XVI reminded the Church many times that for man, authority is often synonymous with possession, dominion, success. For God authority is always synonymous with service, humility, love. It means to enter into Jesus' logic, who bends down to wash the feet of the Apostles (cf. *Angelus*, January 29, 2012), and who says to His disciples: '… [W]hoever would be great among you must be your servant, and whoever would be first among you must be your slave' (cf. *Mt* 20:25–27).

As we can see in Sacred Scripture, mercy is a keyword that indicates God's action towards us. He does not limit Himself merely to affirming His love, but makes it visible and tangible. Love, after all, can never be just an abstraction. By its very nature, it indicates something concrete: intentions, attitudes, and behaviours that are shown in daily living.

—

When we hear the Word of Jesus, when we listen to the Word of Jesus and carry it in our heart, this Word grows. Do you know how it grows? By giving it to the other! The Word of Christ grows in us when we proclaim it, when we give it to others! And this is what Christian life is. It is a mission for the whole Church, for all the baptized, for us all: listen to Jesus and offer Him to others.

Let us enter more deeply into the heart of the Gospel where the poor have a special experience of God's mercy. Jesus introduces us to these works of mercy in His preaching so that we can know whether or not we are living as His disciples. Let us rediscover these corporal works of mercy: to feed the hungry, give drink to the thirsty, clothe the naked, welcome the stranger, heal the sick, visit the imprisoned, and bury the dead.

We find Jesus' wounds in carrying out works of mercy, giving to our body— the body—the soul too, but—I stress—the body of your wounded brother, because he is hungry, because he is thirsty, because he is naked, because he is humiliated, because he is a slave, because he's in jail, because he is in the hospital. Those are the wounds of Jesus today.

Let us ask ourselves—each of us responding in his own heart—let us ask ourselves: Is our faith fruitful? Does our faith produce good works? Or is it sterile instead, and therefore more dead than alive? Do I act as a neighbor or simply pass by? Am I one of those who selects people according to my own liking? It is good to ask ourselves these questions, and to ask them often, because in the end we will be judged on the works of mercy. The Lord will say to us: Do you remember that time on the road from Jerusalem to Jericho? That man who was half dead was me. Do you remember? That hungry child was me. Do you remember? That immigrant who many wanted to drive away, that was me. That grandparent who was alone, abandoned in nursing homes, that was me. That sick man, alone in the hospital, who no one visited, that was me. To live as true children of God means to love our neighbor and to be close to those who are lonely and in difficulty.

Charity is not a simple question of providing assistance, and far less a form of assistance for quieting consciences. No, that is not love, that is sales, that is business. Love is free. Charity and love are a life choice, a way of being, of living, it is the way of humility and solidarity.

The home is a place that teaches charity, a 'school of charity,' which instructs me to go encounter every person, not for profit, but for love.

We cannot escape the Lord's words to us, and they will serve as the criteria upon which we will be judged: whether we have fed the hungry and given drink to the thirsty, welcomed the stranger and clothed the naked, or spent time with the sick and those in prison (cf. *Mt* 25:31–45). Moreover, we will be asked if we have helped others to escape the doubt that causes them to fall into despair and which is often a source of loneliness, if we have helped to overcome the ignorance in which millions of people live, especially children deprived of the necessary means to free them from the bonds of poverty, if we have been close to the lonely and afflicted, if we have forgiven those who have offended us and have rejected all forms of anger and hate that lead to violence, if we have had the kind of patience God shows, who is so patient with us, and if we have commended our brothers and sisters to the Lord in prayer. In each of these 'little ones,' Christ Himself is present. His flesh becomes visible in the flesh of the tortured, the crushed, the scourged, the malnourished, and the exiled … to be acknowledged, touched, and cared for by us. Let us not forget the words of Saint John of the Cross: 'as we prepare to leave this life, we will be judged on the basis of love.'

The most intense joys in life arise when we are able to elicit joy in others, as a foretaste of heaven.

Jesus taught us to be merciful like our heavenly Father (cf. *Lk* 6:36). In the parable of the Good Samaritan (cf. *Lk* 10:29–37), He condemned those who fail to help others in need, those who 'pass by on the other side' (cf. *Lk* 10:31–32). By this example, He taught His listeners, and His disciples in particular, to stop and to help alleviate the sufferings of this world and the pain of our brothers and sisters, using whatever means are at hand, beginning with our own time, however busy we may be.

Let us never forget that authentic power is service, and that the Pope, too, when exercising power, must enter ever more fully into that service which has its radiant culmination on the Cross. He must be inspired by the lowly, concrete, and faithful service which marked Saint Joseph and, like him, he must open his arms to protect all of God's people and embrace with tender affection the whole of humanity, especially the poorest, the weakest, the least important, those whom Matthew lists in the final judgment on love: the hungry, the thirsty, the stranger, the naked, the sick and those in prison (cf. *Mt* 25:31–46). Only those who serve with love are able to protect!

True conversion happens when we accept the gift of grace, and a clear sign of its authenticity is when we become aware of the needs of our brothers and are ready to draw near to them.

Every day we are all called to become a 'caress of God' for those who perhaps have forgotten their first caresses, or perhaps who never have felt a caress in their life.

Sometimes we lose our enthusiasm for mission because we forget that the Gospel responds to our deepest needs, since we were created for what the Gospel offers us: friendship with Jesus and love of our brothers and sisters.

Before all else, the Gospel invites us to respond to the God of love who saves us, to see God in others and to go forth from ourselves to seek the good of others. Under no circumstance can this invitation be obscured! All of the virtues are at the service of this response of love.

Think of the example of Blessed Pier Giorgio Frassati. He said, 'Jesus pays me a visit every morning in Holy Communion, and I return the visit in the meagre way I know how, visiting the poor.' Pier Giorgio was a young man who understood what it means to have a merciful heart that responds to those most in need. He gave them far more than material goods. He gave himself by giving his time, his words, and his capacity to listen.

The Church which 'goes forth' is a community of missionary disciples who take the first step, who are involved and supportive, who bear fruit and rejoice. An evangelizing community knows that the Lord has taken the initiative. He has loved us first (cf. *1 Jn* 4:19), and therefore we can move forward, boldly take the initiative, go out to others, seek those who have fallen away, stand at the crossroads, and welcome the outcast. Such a community has an endless desire to show mercy, the fruit of its own experience of the power of the Father's infinite mercy.

Yes, dear brothers and sisters in Christ, let us all feel closely united to the prayer of our Saviour at the Last Supper, to His appeal: *ut unum sint*. Let us ask the Father of mercies to enable us to live fully the faith graciously bestowed upon us on the day of our Baptism and to bear witness to it freely, joyfully, and courageously. This will be the best service we can offer to the cause of Christian unity, a service of hope for a world still torn by divisions, conflicts, and rivalries. The more we are faithful to His will, in our thoughts, words, and actions, the more we will progress, really and substantially, towards unity.

PART SIX:

*Compassion
through Hospitality*

The danger always remains that by a constant refusal to open the doors of their hearts to Christ who knocks on them in the poor, the proud, rich, and powerful will end up condemning themselves and plunging into the eternal abyss of solitude which is Hell.

When we say 'home' we mean a place of hospitality, a dwelling, a pleasant human environment where one stays readily, finds oneself, feels inserted into a territory, in a community. Yet more profoundly, 'home' is a word with a typically familiar flavor, which recalls warmth, affection, the love that can be felt in a family. Hence the 'home' represents the most precious human treasures, that of encounter, that of relations among people, different in age, culture, and history, but who live together and together help one another to grow. For this reason, the 'home' is a crucial place in life, where life grows and can be fulfilled, because it is a place in which every person learns to receive love and to give love.

A guest doesn't need to be merely served, fed, and cared for in every way ... Above all it is necessary that he is listened to—recall well this word—to listen. That the guest might be welcomed as a person, with his history, his heart rich in sentiments and thoughts, so that he might feel truly that he is among family.

In the Bull of indiction of the Extraordinary Jubilee of Mercy I noted that 'at times we are called to gaze even more attentively on mercy so that we may become a more effective sign of the Father's action in our lives' (*Misericordiae Vultus*, 3). God's love is meant to reach out to each and every person. Those who welcome the Father's embrace, for their part, become so many other open arms and embraces, enabling every person to feel loved like a child and 'at home' as part of the one human family.

And as the door of God's mercy is always open, so too must the doors of our churches, our communities, our parishes, our institutions, our dioceses, be open, because this is how we can all go out to bring this mercy of God.

Compassion, love, is not a vague sentiment, but means taking care of the other, even paying for him. It means compromising oneself, taking all the necessary steps so as to 'approach' the other to the point of identifying with him: 'you shall love your neighbor as yourself.' This is the Lord's Commandment.

We need to go forth from our own communities and be bold enough to go to the existential outskirts that need to feel the closeness of God. He abandons no one, and He always shows His unfailing tenderness and mercy, this, therefore, is what we need to take to all people.

Each of us is responsible for his or her neighbor: we are our brothers' and sisters' keepers, wherever they live. Concern for fostering good relationships with others and the ability to overcome prejudice and fear are essential ingredients for promoting the culture of encounter, in which we are not only prepared to give, but also to receive from others. Hospitality, in fact, grows from both giving and receiving.

Dear brothers and sisters, migrants and refugees! At the heart of the Gospel of mercy the encounter and acceptance by others are intertwined with the encounter and acceptance of God Himself. Welcoming others means welcoming God in person! Do not let yourselves be robbed of the hope and joy of life born of your experience of God's mercy, as manifested in the people you meet on your journey! I entrust you to the Virgin Mary, Mother of migrants and refugees, and to Saint Joseph, who experienced the bitterness of emigration to Egypt. To their intercession I also commend those who invest so much energy, time, and resources to the pastoral and social care of migrants.

The door must protect, of course, but not reject. The door must not be forced but, on the contrary, one asks permission, because hospitality shines in the freedom of welcoming, and dims in the arrogance of invasion. The door is frequently opened, in order to see if there is someone waiting outside, perhaps without the courage nor, perhaps, the strength to knock.

People who pass by, who move on in life without noticing the needs of others, without seeing many spiritual and material needs, are people who pass by without living, they are people who do not need others. Remember well: those who do not live to serve, do not serve to live.

Even in one's own house, among one's own family, it's easier to find service and care of various types than listening ... Today we are so busy and in such a hurry, with so many problems, some of which are unimportant, we lack the capacity to listen. We are constantly busy and thus we don't have time to listen ... You, husband, do you have time to listen to your wife? You, wife, do you have time to listen to your husband? You, parents, do you have time, time to spare, so as to listen to your children, or your grandparents, the elderly? I ask you to learn to listen and dedicate more time to this ... In the capacity to listen is the root of peace.

How often do we encounter a poor person who comes to meet us! We can also be generous, we can have compassion, but usually we do not touch him. We offer him coins, we toss them there, but we avoid touching his hand. And we forget that that person is the Body of Christ! Jesus teaches us not to be afraid to touch the poor and the excluded, because He is in them. Touching the poor can cleanse us from hypocrisy and make us distressed over their condition. Touching the excluded … A Christian excludes no one, gives a place to everyone, allows everyone to come.

Some people prefer not to ask questions or seek answers, they lead lives of comfort, deaf to the cry of those who suffer. Almost imperceptibly, we grow incapable of feeling compassion for others and for their problems, we have no interest in caring for them, as if their troubles were their own responsibility, and none of our business.

The life of Jesus' closest disciples, which is what we are called to be, is shaped by *concrete love*, a love, in other words, marked by *service* and *availability*. It is a life that has no closed spaces or private property for our own use.

Let us try a little harder to take the first step and to become involved. Jesus washed the feet of His disciples. The Lord gets involved and He involves His own, as He kneels to wash their feet ... An evangelizing community gets involved by word and deed in people's daily lives, it bridges distances, it is willing to abase itself if necessary, and it embraces human life, touching the suffering flesh of Christ in others.

Jesus' sacrifice on the cross is nothing else than the culmination of the way He lived His entire life. Moved by His example, we want to enter fully into the fabric of society, sharing the lives of all, listening to their concerns, helping them materially and spiritually in their needs, rejoicing with those who rejoice, weeping with those who weep arm in arm with others, we are committed to building a new world. But we do so not from a sense of obligation, not as a burdensome duty, but as the result of a personal decision which brings us joy and gives meaning to our lives.

We do not live better when we flee, hide, refuse to share, stop giving, and lock ourselves up in our own comforts. Such a life is nothing less than slow suicide.

If we are to share our lives with others and generously give of ourselves, we also have to realize that every person is worthy of our giving. Not for their physical appearance, their abilities, their language, their way of thinking, or for any satisfaction that we might receive, but rather because they are God's handiwork, His creation. God created that person in His image, and he or she reflects something of God's glory. Every human being is the object of God's infinite tenderness, and He Himself is present in their lives. Jesus offered His precious blood on the cross for that person.

My mission of being in the heart of the people is not just a part of my life or a badge I can take off, it is not an 'extra' or just another moment in life. Instead, it is something I cannot uproot from my being without destroying my very self. I am a mission on this earth, that is the reason why I am here in this world. We have to regard ourselves as sealed, even branded, by this mission of bringing light, blessing, enlivening, raising up, healing, and freeing.

May the church be the place of God's mercy and love, where everyone can feel themselves welcomed, loved, forgiven, and encouraged to live according to the good life of the Gospel. And in order to make others feel welcomed, loved, forgiven, and encouraged, the church must have open doors so that all might enter. And we must go out of those doors and proclaim the Gospel.

Are we able to communicate the face of a Church which is 'home' to all? We sometimes speak of a Church that has its doors closed, but here we are contemplating much more than a Church with open doors, much more! ... We need to bring Christ to others, through these joys and hopes, like Mary, who brought Christ to the hearts of men and women, we need to pass through the clouds of indifference without losing our way, we need to descend into the darkest night without being overcome and disoriented, we need to listen to the dreams without being seduced, we need to share their disappointments, without becoming despondent, to sympathize with those whose lives are falling apart without losing our own strength and identity.

Hospitality in families is a crucial virtue today, especially in situations of great poverty, degradation, and domestic violence. Dear brothers and sisters, do not be afraid to invite Jesus to [your] home, that He may be with [you] and safeguard the family. And we mustn't be afraid to also invite His Mother Mary!

PART SEVEN:

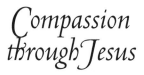

Jesus showed us that the love of God is realized in love for our neighbor. Both go hand-in-hand ... Therefore, this Word of God calls us to love one another, even if we do not always understand each other, and do not always get along ... it is then that Christian love is seen. A love which manifests even if there are differences of opinion or character. Love is greater than these differences!

Jesus teaches us not to be ashamed of touching human misery, of touching His flesh in our brothers and sisters who suffer.

I think we too are the people who, on the one hand, want to listen to Jesus, but on the other hand, at times, like to find a stick to beat others with, to condemn others. And Jesus has this message for us: mercy. I think—and I say it with humility—that this is the Lord's most powerful message: mercy.

With our eyes fixed on Jesus and His merciful gaze, we experience the love of the Most Holy Trinity … This love has now been made visible and tangible in Jesus' entire life. His person is nothing but love, a love given gratuitously…the signs He works, especially in favour of sinners, the poor, the marginalized, the sick, and the suffering, are all meant to teach mercy. Everything in Him speaks of mercy. Nothing in Him is devoid of compassion.

When we stand before Jesus crucified, we see the depth of His love which exalts and sustains us, but at the same time, unless we are blind, we begin to realize that Jesus' gaze, burning with love, expands to embrace all His people. We realize once more that He wants to make use of us to draw closer to His beloved people. He takes us from the midst of His people and He sends us to His people; without this sense of belonging we cannot understand our deepest identity.

Jesus affirms that, from that time onward, the rule of life for His disciples must place mercy at the center, as Jesus Himself demonstrated by sharing meals with sinners.

Jesus' attitude is striking: we do not hear the words of scorn, we do not hear words of condemnation, but only words of love, of mercy, which are an invitation to conversation. 'Neither do I condemn you go, and do not sin again.' Ah! Brothers and Sisters, God's face is the face of a merciful father who is always patient. Have you thought about God's patience, the patience He has with each one of us? That is His mercy. He always has patience, patience with us, He understands us, He waits for us, He does not tire of forgiving us if we are able to return to Him with a contrite heart. 'Great is God's mercy,' says the Psalm.

From the cross, Jesus teaches us how to love even those who do not love us.

I like to remember that title with which the Church Fathers employed in reference to Christ and His work of salvation: *Christus Medicus*. He is the Good Shepherd who cares for the wounded sheep and comforts the sick (cf. *Ez* 34,16), He is the Good Samaritan who does not pass before the badly injured person by the wayside but, moved by compassion, He heals and serves (cf. *Lk* 10.33–34).

God's mercy can make even the driest land become a garden, can restore life to dry bones (cf. *Ez* 37:114) ... Let us be renewed by God's mercy, let us be loved by Jesus, let us enable the power of His love to transform our lives too and let us become agents of this mercy, channels through which God can water the earth, protect all creation, and make justice and peace flourish.

I am always struck when I reread the parable of the merciful Father ... The Father, with patience, love, hope, and mercy, had never for a second stopped thinking about [his wayward son], and as soon as he sees him still far off, he runs out to meet him and embraces him with tenderness, the tenderness of God, without a word of reproach ... God is always waiting for us, He never grows tired. Jesus shows us this merciful patience of God so that we can regain confidence and hope—always!

It is true: the wounds of Jesus are wounds of mercy. 'With His stripes we are healed' (*Is* 53:5). Jesus invites us to behold these wounds, to touch them as Thomas did, to heal our lack of belief. Above all, He invites us to enter into the mystery of these wounds, which is the mystery of His merciful love. Through these wounds, as in a light-filled opening, we can see the entire mystery of Christ and of God: His Passion, His earthly life—filled with compassion for the weak and the sick—His incarnation in the womb of Mary. And we can retrace the whole history of salvation: the prophecies—especially about the Servant of the Lord, the Psalms, the Law, and the Covenant to the liberation from Egypt, to the first Passover and to the blood of the slaughtered lambs and again from the Patriarchs to Abraham, and then all the way back to Abel, whose blood cried out from the earth. All of this we can see in the wounds of Jesus, crucified and risen with Mary, in her Magnificat, we can perceive that, 'His mercy extends from generation to generation' (cf. *Lk* 1:50).

Jesus did not bring hatred, nor did He bring enmity: He brought love—a great love—a heart open to all—to all of us—a love that saves.

We need to help others realize that the only way to encounter others with the right attitude ... is to accept and esteem them as companions along the way, without interior resistance. Better yet, it means learning to find Jesus in the faces of others, in their voices, in their pleas. And learning to suffer in the embrace of the crucified Jesus whenever we are unjustly attacked or meet with ingratitude, never tiring of our decision to live in fraternity.

Jesus, with His cross, walks with us and takes upon Himself our fears, our problems, and our sufferings, even those which are deepest and most painful. With the cross, Jesus unites Himself to the silence of the victims of violence, those who can no longer cry out, especially the innocent and the defenceless. The Cross of Christ bears the suffering and the sin of mankind, including our own. Jesus accepts all this with open arms, bearing on His shoulders our crosses and saying to us: 'Have courage! You do not carry your cross alone! I carry it with you. I have overcome death and I have come to give you hope, to give you life' (*Jn* 3:16).

The world needs Christ more than ever: His salvation, His merciful love. Many people feel an empty void around and within themselves—perhaps, at certain times, we do too; others live in restlessness and insecurity due to uncertainty and conflict. We all need adequate answers to our questions, to our concrete questions. Only in Him, in Christ, is it possible to find true peace and the fulfilment of every human aspiration. Jesus knows the human heart better than anyone. This is why He can heal, giving life and consolation.

After concluding the dialogue with the Apostles, Jesus addressed everyone, saying: 'If anyone wants to come after me, let him deny himself, take up his cross daily and follow me' (v. 23). This is not an ornamental cross or an ideological cross, but it is the cross of life, the cross of one's duty, the cross of making sacrifices for others with love—for parents, for children, for the family, for friends, and even for enemies—the cross of being ready to be in solidarity with the poor, to strive for justice and peace. In assuming this attitude, these crosses, we always lose something. We must never forget that 'whoever loses his life [for Christ] will save it' (v. 24). It is losing in order to win … Jesus, through His Holy Spirit, gives us the strength to move forward along the path of faith and of witness: doing exactly what we believe, not saying one thing and doing another.

Jesus looks beyond the faults and sees the person. He does not halt before bygone evil, but sees future good. His gaze remains constant, even when it is not met it seeks the way of unity and communion. In no case does it halt at appearances, but looks to the heart. With this gaze of Jesus, you can help bring about another humanity, without looking for acknowledgement but seeking goodness for its own sake, content to maintain a pure heart and to fight peaceably for honesty and justice.

Dear brothers and sisters, the Lord never tires of having mercy on us, and wants to offer us His forgiveness once again—we all need it—inviting us to return to Him with a new heart, purified of evil, purified by tears, to take part in His joy.

With our eyes fixed on Jesus and His merciful gaze, we experience the love of the Most Holy Trinity ... His person is nothing but love, a love given gratuitously. The relationships He forms with the people who approach Him manifest something entirely unique and unrepeatable. The signs He works, especially in favor of sinners, the poor, the marginalized, the sick, and the suffering, are all meant to teach mercy. Everything in Him speaks of mercy. Nothing in Him is devoid of compassion.

The Church is commissioned to announce the mercy of God, the beating heart of the Gospel, which in its own way must penetrate the heart and mind of every person. The Spouse of Christ must pattern her behavior after the Son of God who went out to everyone without exception.

This Holy Year will bring to the fore the richness of Jesus' mission echoed in the words of the prophet: to bring a word and gesture of consolation to the poor, to proclaim liberty to those bound by new forms of slavery in modern society, to restore sight to those who can see no more because they are caught up in themselves, to restore dignity to all those from whom it has been robbed.

Faced with the tragic events of human history we can feel crushed at times, asking ourselves, 'Why?' Humanity's evil can appear in the world like an abyss, a great void: empty of love, empty of goodness, empty of life. And so we ask: how can we fill this abyss? For us it is impossible, only God can fill this emptiness that evil brings to our hearts and to human history. It is Jesus, God-made man, who died on the Cross and who fills the abyss of sin with the depth of His mercy.

May the Father's merciful gaze touch and help us to welcome our poverty in order to move forward with faith, and to commit ourselves together to a 'revolution of tenderness'. This is a challenge for you: bring about a revolution of tenderness. Regarding this revolution, Jesus opened the way to us through His Incarnation. It is beautiful to be His missionary disciples who console, enlighten, soothe, set free, and guide.

In Jesus His Son, God has come down among us. He took flesh and showed His solidarity with humanity in all things but sin. Jesus identified with us: He became 'the firstborn among many brethren' (*Rom* 8:29). He was not content merely to teach the crowds, but He was concerned for their welfare, especially when He saw them hungry (cf. *Mk* 6:34–44) or without work (cf. *Mt* 20:3). He was concerned not only for men and women, but also for the fish of the sea, the birds of the air, plants and trees, all things great and small. He saw and embraced all of creation.

You are the visible face of the invisible Father, of the God who manifests His power above all by forgiveness and mercy: let the Church be your visible face in the world, its Lord risen and glorified.

The life of Jesus is a life for others. It is a life of service.

Jesus did more than just see, He touched people's lives, He spoke to them, helped them, and showed kindness to those in need. Not only this, but He felt strong emotions and He wept (cf. *Jn* 11:33–44). And He worked to put an end to suffering, sorrow, misery, and death. The Gospel of the healing of the leper tells us today that, if we want to be true disciples of Jesus, we are called to become united to Him, instruments of His merciful love, overcoming every kind of marginalization. In order to be 'imitators of Christ' (cf. I *Cor* 11:1) in the face of a poor or sick person, we must not be afraid to look him in the eye and to draw near with tenderness and compassion, and to touch him and embrace him. I have often asked this of people who help others, to do so looking them in the eye, not to be afraid to touch them, that this gesture of help may also be a gesture of communication: we too need to be welcomed by them. A gesture of tenderness, a gesture of compassion ... Let us ask you: when you help others, do you look them in the eye? Do you embrace them without being afraid to touch them? Do you embrace them with tenderness? Think about this: how do you help? From a distance or with tenderness, with closeness?

Following Jesus demands a good dose of courage, a readiness to trade in the sofa for a pair of walking shoes and to set out on new and uncharted paths. To blaze trails that open up new horizons capable of spreading joy, the joy that is born of God's love and wells up in your hearts with every act of mercy. To take the path of the 'craziness' of our God, who teaches us to encounter Him in the hungry, the thirsty, the naked, the sick,

the friend in trouble, the prisoner, the refugee
and the migrant, and our neighbors who feel
abandoned. To take the path of our God,
who encourages us to be politicians, thinkers,
social activists. The God who asks us to devise
an economy inspired by solidarity. In all the
settings in which you find yourselves, God's
love invites you bring the Good News, making
of your own lives a gift to Him and to others.

At the foot of the Cross, Mary, together with John, the disciple of love, witnessed the words of forgiveness spoken by Jesus. This supreme expression of mercy towards those who crucified Him show us the point to which the mercy of God can reach. Mary attests that the mercy of the Son of God knows no bounds and extends to everyone, without exception. Let us address her in the words of the *Salve Regina*, a prayer ever ancient and ever new, so that she may never tire of turning her merciful eyes upon us, and make us worthy to contemplate the face of mercy, her Son Jesus.

Our Lord's mercy can be seen especially when He bends down to human misery and shows His compassion for those in need of understanding, healing, and forgiveness. Everything in Jesus speaks of mercy. Indeed, He Himself *is* mercy.

PART EIGHT

Pope Francis on Compassion

This particular full address by Pope Francis was selected as representative of his Gospel-led, pastoral-driven, and Jesus-centred belief in the centrality of compassion to the life of a Christian. In introducing this collection of 250 of his quotes on this theme, the text provides a more complete expression of the Holy Father's perspective on and advocacy for compassion. It was delivered by Pope Francis at the General Audience in Saint Peter's Square on Wednesday, 27 April 2016.

Dear Brothers and Sisters, good morning! Today let us reflect on the parable of the Good Samaritan (*Lk* 10:25–37). A doctor of the Law puts Jesus to the test with this question: 'Teacher, what shall I do to inherit eternal life?' (v. 25). Jesus asks him to answer the question Himself, and the man answers perfectly: 'You shall love the Lord your God with all your heart, and with all your soul, and with all your strength, and with all your mind; and your neighbor as yourself' (v. 27). Jesus then concludes: 'Do this, and you will live' (v. 28).

Then the man asks another question, which is very meaningful for us: 'Who is my neighbor?' (v. 29), and he emphasizes, 'my relatives? my compatriots? Those of my religion?' Thus, he wants a clear rule that allows him to classify others as 'neighbor' and 'non-neighbor,' as those who can become neighbors and those who cannot become neighbors.

Jesus responds with a parable, taking the example of a priest, a Levite, and a Samaritan. The first two are figures linked to Temple worship; the third is a schismatic Jew, considered a stranger, pagan and impure, namely the Samaritan. On the road from Jerusalem to Jericho the priest and the Levite come upon a dying man, whom robbers have attacked, stripped, and abandoned. The Law of the Lord in similar situations imposes the duty to assist him, but both pass by without stopping. They were in a hurry... The priest, perhaps, looked at his watch and said 'I am late for Mass... I must say Mass.' The other may have said: 'I don't know if the Law permits me to, because there is blood there and I will be impure...' They take another way and do not approach him. Here the parable offers us the first lesson: those who attend the house of God and know His mercy do not automatically know how to love their neighbor. It is not automatic! You may know the whole Bible, you may know all the liturgical rubrics, you may know all theology, but from this knowledge love is not automatic: loving has another path, it requires intelligence, but also something more…The priest and the Levite see but ignore; they look but they do not offer to help. Yet there is no true worship if it is not translated into service to a neighbor. Let us never forget this: before the suffering of so many people exhausted by hunger, violence, and injustice, we cannot remain spectators.

What does it mean to ignore the suffering of man? It means to ignore God! If I do not draw close to that man, that woman, that child, that elderly man or woman who are suffering, I do not draw close to God.

Let us come to the core of the parable: the Samaritan, namely the despised man, the one whom no one would have bet on, and who also had his own commitments and things to do. When he saw the wounded man, he did not pass by like the other two, who were linked to the Temple, but 'he had compassion' (v. 33). Thus the Gospel says: 'He had compassion,'

that is, his heart, his emotions, were moved!
This is the difference. The other two 'saw,'
but their hearts remained closed, cold. While
the Samaritan was in synchrony with the
very heart of God. Indeed, 'compassion' is an
essential characteristic of God's mercy. God
has compassion on us. What does this mean?
He suffers with us, He feels our suffering.
Compassion means 'suffer with.' The verb
indicates that the physique is moved and
trembles at the sight of the evil of man. In the
gestures and deeds of the Good Samaritan we
recognize the merciful acts of God in all of
salvation history. It is the same compassion

with which the Lord comes to meet each one of us: He does not ignore us, He knows our pain, He knows how much we need help and comfort. He comes close and never abandons us. Each of us ask and answer the question in our heart: 'Do I believe? Do I believe that the Lord has compassion on me, just as I am, a sinner, with many problems and many issues?' Think about that and the answer is: 'Yes!' But each one must see in his heart whether he has faith in this compassion of God, of the good God who draws close, heals us, caresses us. If we reject Him, He waits: He is patient and is always beside us.

The Samaritan acts with true mercy: he binds up that man's wounds, takes him to an inn, takes care of him personally, and provides for his care. All this teaches us that compassion, love, is not a vague sentiment, but means taking care of the other, even paying for him. It means compromising oneself, taking all the necessary steps so as to 'approach' the other to the point of identifying with him: 'you shall love your neighbour as yourself.' This is the Lord's Commandment.

When the parable ends, Jesus reverses the question of the doctor of the Law, and asks him: 'Which of these three, do you think, proved neighbor to the man who fell among the robbers?' (v. 36). The response is completely unequivocal: 'The one who showed mercy on him' (v. 37). At the beginning of the parable, for the priest and the Levite, the neighbor was the dying man. At the end, the neighbor is the Samaritan who drew near. Jesus reverses the perspective: do not stand by classifying others by sight who is neighbor and who is not. You can become neighbor to any needy person you meet, and you will know that you have compassion in your heart, that is, whether you have the capacity to suffer with the other.

This parable is a splendid gift for us all, and also a task! To each of us Jesus repeats what He said to the doctor of the Law: 'Go and do likewise' (v. 37). We are all called to follow the same path of the Good Samaritan, who is the figure of Christ: Jesus bent down to us, He became our servant, and thus He has saved us, so that we too might love as He loved us, in the same way.

GO AND DO LIKEWISE (CF *LK* 10, 25–37)

PART NINE

Reader's Journal

A Note on the Reader's Journal

'God has compassion on us. What does this mean? He suffers with us, He feels our suffering. Compassion means "suffer with."'

'We are all called to follow the same path of the Good Samaritan, who is the figure of Christ: Jesus bent down to us, He became our servant, and thus He has saved us, so that we too might love as He loved us, in the same way.'

Pope Francis

The following pages of the reader's journal offer a space for reflection on these words by Pope Francis. We might ask ourselves how we have recognized God's compassion in our lives and in the lives of others, how we in turn have imitated the Good Samaritan and have shown compassion to our neighbors, from our very own family members to strangers we pass on the street. In what way do we express that compassion? Do we 'suffer with' others in a way that is loving, humble, merciful, and tender or in a way that is resentful or prideful?

Entering into suffering with others gives us the freedom to forget ourselves and to acknowledge the brokenness in all of us that only God can heal. As Pope Francis has attested to in both word and deed, when we do this we open ourselves up to God's grace and we are transfigured. People really change. Relationships are really mended. We then not only believe in God's love, but we experience it for ourselves.

'Situations can change; people can change. Be the first to seek to bring good. Do not grow accustomed to evil, but defeat it with good.'

Pope Francis

Sample Questions for Reflection

Whom have I helped recently?

Whom have I spoken a kind word to?

Whom have I treated with patience?

How do I respond to the needy, the poor, hungry, sick, elderly, or lonely?

Do I seek and accept forgiveness from others, and from God?

About the Editors

Andrea Kirk Assaf has had the rare privilege of covering three pontificates in the span of a decade: the pontificates of John Paul II, Benedict XVI, and Francis. In 2002 she moved to Rome to write for *Inside the Vatican* magazine and several other Catholic and secular news outlets, covering World Youth Day in Toronto, the funeral of John Paul II,

the election of Pope Benedict XVI, and
now the popularity of the first successor of
St Peter from the New World, Pope Francis.
Along with her editor-journalist-translator
husband, Tony Assaf, and their three
children, Andrea divides her days between
the Eternal City of Rome, Italy, and a rural
homestead in Remus, Michigan, U.S.A.

Kelly Anne Leahy graduated from Villanova University, in Pennsylvania, U.S.A., in 2014. Upon graduation, she traveled to Kolkata, India, to volunteer as a teacher for disabled children with Mother Teresa's Missionaries of Charity. Shortly after returning from India, Kelly moved to Rome, Italy, and had the opportunity to meet Pope Francis at a conference in the Vatican.

In a room full of approximately 250 people, he stopped to greet each one individually, demonstrating the power of even the briefest loving encounter. Inspired by her work with the Missionaries of Charity and Pope Francis' call to active compassion for the poor, Kelly Anne is currently launching her own organization to benefit children living on the streets in Kolkata.